PENGUIN BOOKS

BESSIE SMITH

Elaine Feinstein is a poet and novelist. Her most recent novel, *The Border*, was published in paperback in 1985, and her latest book of poems, *People*, will be published in spring 1986. She is at present working on a screenplay of her novel *The Crystal Garden*.

LIVES OF MODERN WOMEN

General Editor: Emma Tennant

Lives of Modern Women is a series of short biographical portraits by distinguished writers of significant twentieth-century women whose lives, ideas, struggles and creative talents contributed something new to a world in transition.

It is hoped that both the fascination of comparing the aims, ideals, set-backs and achievements of our grandmothers' generation with our own and the high quality of writing and insight will encourage the reader to delve further into the lives and works of those who have helped carve out a more acceptable and challenging place in society for the women of today.

Elaine Feinstein

Bessie Smith

Penguin Books

For Martin

Penguin Books Ltd, Harmondsworth, Middlesex, England
Viking Penguin Inc., 40 West 23rd Street, New York, New York 10010, U.S.A.
Penguin Books Australia Ltd, Ringwood, Victoria, Australia
Penguin Books Canada Ltd, 2801 John Street, Markham, Ontario, Canada L3R 1B4
Penguin Books (N.Z.) Ltd, 182–190 Wairau Road, Auckland 10, New Zealand

First published 1985
Published simultaneously by Viking

Made and printed in Great Britain by
Richard Clay (The Chaucer Press) Ltd,
Bungay, Suffolk
Typeset in Monophoto Photina

CONTENTS

LIST OF PLATES

1894(?) Bessie Smith is born in Chattanooga,
         Tennessee. The date is the one given on her
         1923 marriage certificate.

1912   Bessie joins the Moses Stokes travelling show.

1913   Bessie begins to travel around the South with her
         own act.

1917   First jazz records made.

1920   Eighteenth amendment prohibiting
         manufacture, sale and consumption of alcohol.

1922   Bessie meets Jack Gee.

1923   Bessie makes her first record with Columbia.
         Bessie marries Jack Gee.

1929   Wall Street Crash.
         Talkies firmly established.
         Alberta Hunt stars in *Showboat* with Paul Robeson
         in London.
         Ethel Waters stars at the London Palladium.

1931   Bessie is dropped by Columbia records.

1935   Billie Holiday and Ella Fitzgerald open at the Apollo.

1937   Bessie dies in a car accident.

ONE

In her song nothing melts, yields or seduces. Her voice is harsh and coarse, undeterred by everything she knows about touring in tents, street fights and casual sex. She isn't trying to please anyone. The habit of submission, of letting yourself be used, comes too easily to women. In Bessie's voice is a full-hearted rejection of any such foolishness. The strength to do so comes from the big voice itself, with the growl and rasp of a jazz trumpet in it.

Her phrasing is unhurried and subtle. She knows exactly where to place an extra syllable, where to stress a word. And always, under the sadness, lie a sense of freedom and the triumph of her own courageous spirit.

On long-haul drives across country it is Bessie's voice I hear in my ears as I make up my own songs to her music. Her lonely voice opposes a stubborn pride to the ordinary injustice of men.

And bawdy lyrics, delivered with gaiety, are as much a part of her message as the stoicism of the blues. They don't flatter men, for all their desperate insistence on a share of the male 'jelly roll'. On the contrary, the playfulness is the counterpart of men's most arrogant interest in women. The heroines of her lyrics are Amazonian and Junoesque, indefatigably sexual; her voice and Louis' trumpet exchange brazen and derisive comment.

'Once I lived the life of a millionaire.' So begins the song most closely linked to Bessie's name. Bessie never was a millionaire, but for the six years or so in which she made large sums of money she lived exactly as she would have done if she had been. She never saved or invested or acquired much property. The things she enjoyed buying were for immediate consumption, or gifts. She loved spending money on jewellery or clothes for herself or her husband, or even giving her dollars away, to her family, old friends down on their luck or strangers. And when she went out drinking, she liked to give a drink to everyone in the bar.

She had no interest in making a home in any of the flats or houses she rented as her main base. She could have afforded to buy any furniture she wanted, but she was satisfied with comfortable sofas and chairs. Home wasn't the place in which she felt most herself.

Her single most extravagant acquisition was characteristically on the move with her and her show: a custom-built, brightly painted railroad car made for her by the Southern Iron and Equipment Company in Atlanta. It was large enough to carry her whole show on their travels. Seventy-eight feet long and built on two storeys, it was altogether magnificently appointed; but it was functional, not a folly, because there were many small towns which had no hotel in which to house her troupe. They could live on the train instead, since there was a kitchen and a bathroom, hot and cold water, and plenty of room for everyone to relax or have parties. The train was her brother Clarence's idea, but it altogether fitted Bessie's idea of luxury, which was to be unrooted and Empress of her own domain.

Bessie played in theatres from Memphis to Chicago and New York, and wherever she went her voice declared her determination to live as fully as possible.

I'm a young woman and ain't done running aroun'.
Some people call me hobo, some people call me bum,
Nobody knows my name, nobody knows what I've done.

I'm as good as anyone in your town.
I ain't a high yellow, I'm a deep yellow brown.
I ain't gonna marry, ain't gonna settle down,
I'm gonna drink good moonshine, and run these browns
　　down.

Bessie's size impressed her audience, because she learnt to use it. When she first went to Frank Walker's studio in Columbia in 1924, she was awkwardly 'tall, fat and scared to death', but she could already dominate a stage. Her bulk became a massive fact there, overwhelming her listeners with a sense of her majesty even as they recognized their own pain in her voice. On stage she was 'a *big* woman, with that beautiful bronze colour and stern features, stately, just like a queen', as Zutty Singleton remembers her (quoted in Hentoff and Shapiro's *Hear Me Talkin' to Ya*).

Blues were always associated with a lack of manners, and Bessie did not change that. She did give the association a new meaning. The roughness became formidable and the lack of social acceptability became defiance. On-stage, that combination was triumphal. Off-stage it remained alarming. When May Wright, a blues singer whose husband, James P. Johnson, played piano for Bessie, says of her (Hentoff and Shapiro, op. cit.) while declaring no one could sing as well as she did, 'Mind you, she wasn't a friend of mine. She was very rough', it is a certain remembered apprehension that comes through, rather than snobbery.

Alberta Hunter, one of Bessie's finest contemporaries, knew that 'Bessie was the greatest of them all. Even though she was raucous and loud. She had a sort of tear – no, not a tear, but there was a *misery* in what she did.' That ability to infect the audience not so much with her own misery, but with a sudden knowledge of their own unhappiness, was the secret of Bessie's power: 'You didn't turn your head when she was on. She just upset you' (Hentoff and Shapiro, op. cit.).

If I try to conjure up Bessie's presence, in wig and

feathers, ready to go on stage, she rises before me, a large-framed woman, with a quick temper, used to resorting to violence when crossed. She was strong enough to fell a man; and she didn't always wait to be attacked before using her fists.

I don't want to be prissy about this physical fury, which came out of her early days on Chattanooga streets, and was part of black ghetto life. Her use of her fists was akin to the obscenity of her ordinary speech; and she never allowed success to modify her behaviour in any way. But if I had met Bessie, cruising round her streets, I might not have recognized her great spirit, and she might have disliked my white skin, long face and skinny figure. I should like to have told her that her voice has given me courage. Perhaps she would have understood. I'm not her only unlikely admirer, nor even the unlikeliest. Perhaps I could explain that nearly half a century after her death we still take fire when we listen to her.

TWO

The voice of early city blues is female for the most part; men sang the great field songs and took their country blues along the back roads of the South; but Ma Rainey, Bessie Smith and Ethel Waters had a new provenance. They sang about the ills at the heart of women's lives: their dependence on luck, their dependence on men and their efforts to cope with betrayal and desertion.

Women in the United States won the vote in 1920 but the situation of black women hardly changed. How could it? Black women were the bottom of the pile. They were exploited by the whole of society, consigned to the role of mammy or whore, or forced out to work by lonely necessity. A woman who had a partner who stayed with her (and many left home) was often brutally abused. A black man was likely to be so abominably treated in all his other relationships that he found it impossible to react humanly. Black women fell into the habit of thinking of their men as lazy, shiftless and irresponsible.

Bessie's lyric makes the point humorously enough, but it was a bitter world in which that joke was lived out:

There's nineteen men live in my neighbourhood.
There nineteen men live in my neighbourhood.
Eighteen of them are fools, and the one ain't no doggone
     good.

This is the emotional reality that underlies the blues. As the folklorists Odum and Johnson, writing about the catalogues of 'race' records from three major companies, observed in 1926 (in *Negro Workaday Songs*): 'The majority of formal blues are sung from the point of view of women . . . Among the blues singers who have gained national recognition there is scarcely a man's name to be found.'

And the songs were repeated by prostitutes standing in their little-girl dresses in the doorways of their shacks in the South, or mothers hanging over their children at night. Alberta Hunter explained: 'The blues? why the blues are part of me . . . when we sing the blues we're singing out our hearts, we're singing out our feelings. Maybe we're hurt and just can't answer back, then we sing and even hum the blues . . . When I sing:

I walk the floor

Yes, I walk the floor, wringing my hands, and cry.

what I'm doing is letting my soul out' (Hentoff and Shapiro, op. cit.).

Women always loved the Southern Church, because their life was painfully ugly, and the shared communion was necessary to them. The Southern Baptist's hymns could transmute the meanest experience into glory, and women rocked to the rhythm of the songs with cries of ecstasy and recognition. The Church may have disliked the blues, because people listened to them in low dives while they were drinking and playing cards, but a similar fervour inspired the singing of both hymns and songs. And the raunchiest performers had religious thoughts. Ma Rainey turned to God towards the end of her life. Ethel Waters sang for Billy Graham. Even Bessie liked to go to Church on a Sunday, though it doesn't seem to have acted as a brake on her behaviour, and she had none of the piety of Ethel Waters. The reverence was for life and love; acceptance of a life that was very often painfully ugly was transmuted in the communion of the music.

There is nothing in my own soft early years to help me grasp what it meant to be black and poor as Bessie was in her childhood. She was born in the railroad town of

Chattanooga, Tennessee, in 1894, one of seven children of William Smith, a part-time Baptist preacher. The whole family lived in poverty, which remained an inescapable fact of black life even though nearly thirty years had gone by since the end of slavery on the Day of Jubilo. The eldest son of the family died before Bessie was born, and her father soon after. Her mother was dead by the time she was eight. Bessie and the other surviving children were brought up by the eldest sister, Viola. There was little money for food, and none for doctors; no interest in schooling; and not much chance of finding a job of any kind. Half of Chattanooga was black and facing the same problems, so there was no easy way out of the ghetto.

From the age of nine, Bessie sang on street corners for nickels; she had a naturally powerful voice, and her earnings made a useful contribution to the family needs. She sang everything, including Baptist hymns, with the same healthy exuberance. There was a good deal of enterprise in the Smith family; it was Clarence who first succeeded in joining Moses Stokes's travelling show as a dancer and comedian. In 1912 he arranged for Bessie to have an audition. By then she would have been about eighteen, and, to judge by the photographs, touchingly eager and vulnerable, in spite of her years on the Chattanooga streets learning to look after herself. Apart from reading and writing she had learnt very little else.

The audition brought Bessie the first luck she had,

because the cast included Gertrude Rainey and her husband, Will. Aside from the chance this gave Bessie to listen and learn from Ma Rainey, Mother of the Blues, this was the first time a jazz singer of high calibre had heard her sing. And when the Raineys broke away to join another troupe a few months later, Bessie went with them. Ma Rainey had no children of her own, and she treated Bessie like a daughter, which made it easy for Bessie to leave her family.

Ma Rainey was a short, stubby figure, who loved dressing up outrageously: she loaded herself with diamonds and gold. She took particular pleasure in a necklace of gold coins, of different sizes, from $2.50 to heavy $20 eagles, which she often kept on in bed for fear it would get stolen. Her face was kindly; and her smile, too, was benevolent, even though her large teeth were capped with gold, and there was something in her which frightened men. Ma preferred her own sex.

'Boy, she was the horriblest-looking thing I ever seen,' Little Brother Montgomery reported.

She was a good person to work for none the less. She wasn't a soft touch for money if one of her troupe had lost his own while gambling, any more than Bessie was; but if someone was in trouble she helped out quickly enough. When someone asked her whether she had any money, she replied with a laugh that rumbled through her whole body, 'Honey chile, what you talkin' about? I got a roll big enough to choke on' (quoted in

Derrick S. Baxter's *Ma Rainey and the Classic Blues Singers*).

Her voice is the closest to Bessie's in power; her long drawn-out *Hmmmmmmm* as sensuous. Ma's earthy, rural quality, which recalls wandering hobo singers, was too rough for the Northern audiences. She did not often perform north of Virginia.

Ma didn't need to kidnap Bessie to get her out of Chattanooga, as some stories suggest. Bessie was already weary with wanting to get away. And she understood that it was only by leaving that she could help support her sisters, and the children they already had. It was a financial contribution she was to make, ungrudgingly, for the rest of her life.

To succeed in the entertainment business of the time, Bessie's most significant disadvantages were her size, the African cast of her features and the unfashionable blackness of her skin. The chorus line was expected to look as if tanned golden-brown and to have a slender build; and beauty was supposed to lie in small, European features. Bessie's early full-lipped loveliness was unacceptable. Irvin C. Miller (himself black) had her thrown out of the chorus line for not meeting these standards, which must have bruised her awakening confidence, but did not check her determination. The scar remained, and probably accounts for her lifelong dislike of 'Northern bitches' with skins much lighter than her own. People have to love themselves if they are going to survive, and Bessie was a survivor. If she was black, then black was good. And all her life she preferred men who were as dark a black as she was.

Bessie's empire extended more widely than Ma's, but she never aspired to widen it in the way Ethel Waters was able to. At the height of her fame Bessie played to white audiences in the South, as well as in night clubs in the North, but never saw the white audience as an opportunity. Ethel Waters was sharper about what was to her advantage. It was partly because she came from the North, and was bewildered to find how much blacks in the South were afraid to seem uppity. It was partly because of her mixed blood, which explains her physical features. But she was also a very different personality.

Ethel was a singer with talent; she was also pretty and (for much of her life) slender; hence her nickname, 'Sweet Mama Stringbean'. Her own childhood was lonelier than Bessie's; since she was the result of a rape, her mother regarded her with hostility for all her prettiness and intelligence. Born in a slum in Chester, Pennsylvania, she was brought face to face with poverty and squalor at least equal to anything in Bessie's childhood. But her grandmother was hard-working and determined that she wanted a better life for her children. It was her voice which urged Ethel towards cleanliness and moderation in her drinking. It was her grandmother who taught her to imagine God's eye on her. And although her temper was as violent as Bessie's in her childhood, and she was familiar with local whores and all the crime and vice of a slum ghetto, she had more interest in her schooling than Bessie.

Ethel Waters went on to star in Broadway musicals, and to act in Hollywood. Neither world opened to Bessie. People close to Bessie say this was because she did not want to leave her own people. But Ethel Waters, too, preferred black audiences initially. She liked the way they ran up and down the aisles, yelling greetings to friends and sometimes fighting. Her first appearance before a white audience appalled her because of its restraint. She thought she was a failure, because they received her only by clapping their hands. But once she understood their different style and decided what they liked about her was her soft voice and sweetness, she determined to give them what they wanted. She never liked the appurtenances of white life that went along with success, such as caviare and expensive European food, but she enjoyed the success. And even though she found many white people joyless, she liked the society of successful writers, and was able to discuss books with them and ideas for interpreting roles.

Bessie was more intelligent musically than Ethel Waters. No one can listen to her immaculate phrasing without understanding that. Yet there was a whole range of intelligence she chose not to use, or perhaps lacked.

It was not fortuitous that Ethel opened her act with

which she toured in her early days by being called on stage and identifying herself with the catch-phrase, 'Well, I'm not Bessie Smith', which brought a laugh. She made herself the deliberate antithesis of all Bessie stood for although off-stage she shared much of Bessie's refusal to be pushed around.

Bessie sensed this opposition instinctively, and was jealous of her. She could forgive prettiness in singers who were altogether inferior to her in musical power, and she could forgive talent as long as it did not threaten her on her own territory. When Ethel Waters came to appear at the '91' club in Atlanta early in her career, Bessie insisted that if she was going to appear on the same bill she wasn't allowed to sing blues songs.

Ethel Waters did not hold this against Bessie, in whom she recognized both spirit and greatness. And she did not challenge Bessie, though she was willing to fight hand to hand herself. She had a much stronger need to be liked than Bessie. It was only in the world of show business that she found solace and camaraderie.

Bessie loved the world of tent-shows. Being on the road was something which gave her a chance to do what she liked, which was particularly sweet to someone who had been pinned for the first eighteen years of her life in Chattanooga. Blacks were willing to sacrifice a lot for that freedom, as Mark Twain noted years earlier, when he suggested that the appetite had a root in the privations of slavery: 'They stay on a plantation 'til the desire to travel seizes them; then they pack up, hail a steamboat and clear out.' Odum and Johnson noted as much of the hobo singer in 1925: 'He makes much of his hard time, his lack of friends and sympathy ... [But] he makes conditions of his own liking, and these conditions constitute his good time.' And so Bessie enjoyed the camaraderie of her touring days with the Rabbit Foot Minstrels, a troupe managed by F. C. Wolcott. She was to tour in much more glamorous conditions; but from the beginning she liked the life and had no desire to settle down in one place. Ethel Waters, who was also in a tent-show, remembers sleeping in a stable because the coloured people in Lexington, Kentucky, wouldn't let carnival showgirls sleep in their rooms, but even on the road she had her eye on the advantage of a fixed place to live. She did not enjoy the riotous living of tours, and always refused to drink alcohol. It was her kind of integrity.

Bessie's strength was more inward, as Sidney Bechet ruminates about her, in *Treat It Gentle*: 'The great person, he's the one who takes all of those influences [of people or music], gives them what he's got inside him, and he expresses that.' What Bessie had inside her was an impatience with the whole of the white world.

Ida Cox, whose career covers much of the same territory, and who also began singing with the Rabbit Foot Minstrels, sang rather as Bessie might have done of disliking those who were Northern yellow, and she too claimed that Southern men were likely to be more loyal than those from the North.

THREE

Bessie carried herself as if she did not know how old she was, and felt beautiful, and liked her own size, in the same way that she wore her blackness with pride instinctively and before it was fashionable. This made her an ideal figure for Amira Baraka (Leroi Jones) to centre his *Blues People* upon, though it is a book from a frenetic decade, the sixties, which has slipped away.

Her shout of rage, which issues in violence or the insolent admonition to 'kiss her black ass', remains a magnificent symbol of her obstinate belief in herself, even though the very qualities which make her a splendid symbol of resistance to white definitions damaged her own choices. And there may always be a paradox while urban blacks continue for the most part to live so much more poorly than fellow Americans. The hopelessness of the black ghettos in the United States now is frightening. At the same time, black talent is felt everywhere in America. The liveliness and confidence of writers and musicians, university professors and television comedians, is a delight. It is hard to say that blacks should turn their back on the white world.

In many ways the North has gone further wrong than the South for all the terror of the sixties and the brutality of those who opposed the civil rights movement. Black poets or novelists report their astonishment at finding greater understanding for blacks in the Southern States than in the North. It seems as if once the barriers were down, and the possibility of maintaining segregation had gone, the greater homeliness and familiarity of a culture so permeated with the influence of blacks became most hospitable to them.

Bessie's life-long defiance of the white world, which included a rejection of its most plausible invitations, went back to her childhood in a completely racist South. She had no expectation of making herself acceptable then, and her contempt for those who tried to conform was profound. Later in life her income would have enabled her to live in style with other successful black entertainers on Long Island, but she had no desire to join them. She would have had to pretend; and to do that would have changed her whole being. The black word for those who took on a white style of life was *dicty*, and Bessie never used the word without dislike.

In turn, successful blacks disliked Bessie, because they felt her behaviour endangered their own image of themselves. The crudity of her language, and the unpredictability of her moods, made her seem like a part of the street life they wanted to forget. Bessie continued to enjoy that life: its food, its home-made liquor and its uninhibited parties. Essentially, she was refusing to acknowledge the class system the blacks had set up which put the white world at the unreachable top of the tree. She knew it was a system which had rejected her once and for all when she was thrown out of the chorus line for having too dark a skin. She knew it was a system that would draw back in disapproval if she behaved naturally. She was impatient of such constraints. As she sang in 'T'aint Nobody's Biz-ness If I Do'

There ain't nothin' I can do, or nothin' I can say, that
    folks don't criticize me.
But I'm going to do just as I want to anyway and don't
    care if they all despise me.

Bessie had many white admirers of her singing who were eager to entertain her, but she never felt comfortable in their homes. In the ordinary sense of the word they didn't make her nervous; but she felt her size and her blackness sharply in their company. That is why she often behaved with deliberate vulgarity.

Carl Van Vechten was a rich young journalist whose interest in black writers and musicians had done a good deal to bring them to the attention of the American public. He often held parties in his Manhattan flat which introduced them to the leading figures of the

New York cultural élite. One evening in 1928 he invited Bessie.

It was not the kind of occasion that Bessie relished, and she only accepted the invitation because the composer of *Mississippi Days*, her current show, asked her to do so. Porter Grainger, the composer, was an elegantly dressed young man whose self-esteem depended a great deal on his contacts in the smart white world. Bessie made fun of this often, but she liked him nevertheless, and although he was homosexual had occasionally slept with him.

The evening's disaster showed Bessie at her unrepentant worst. She arrived like an empress, in ermine and much bejewelled, and at once realized she was on alien territory, however much Van Vechten tried to welcome her. Her dismay took the form of rudeness as she was scrutinized curiously by the staring white faces around her.

When Bessie was embarrassed, she took refuge in being offensive. That way she pre-empted unfavourable judgement. So when Van Vechten offered her a Martini she rejected it and demanded a whiskey, and as her friend Ruby fussed with a dangling mink coat she took pleasure in swearing at her to take the damned thing off. Porter Grainger, who had arrived with Bessie and Ruby, tried to pretend nothing out of the way was happening.

Van Vechten asked Bessie to sing while Grainger accompanied her on the piano. This part of the evening at least went well. Bessie transformed the strange faces into a group she could handle like any other audience once she began to sing. Van Vechten recorded his triumphant sense of a memorable occasion in an article he wrote for *Jazz Record* two decades later, in which he describes the ferocity of her singing with admiration. What he chose not to mention was the way she had been drinking all through her performance; or her behaviour as it ended and Grainger tried to hustle her into leaving.

Even as Grainger urged Bessie toward the door her hostess tried to stop and embrace her. This ill-fated gesture led to a convulsive rejection by Bessie, who knocked her over as she threw off the polite arms, saying: 'Get the fuck away from me. I never heard of such shit.'

The acceptable language of polite society was a good deal less open to four-letter words than it would be today. And it took considerable aplomb for Van Vechten to help his wife to her feet, and escort an irritable Bessie to the elevator, civilly.

Carl Van Vechten behaved remarkably well, and was a finer man altogether than Bessie recognized. His admiration for Bessie was enough to secure his understanding, and he knew a great deal about black life. Ethel Waters made a good friend of both him and his wife, though she had as little liking as Bessie for the beautiful objects Carl collected in his flat. She found his novel *Nigger Heaven* (in spite of a title she hated) a sympathetic and accurate study of the way blacks were forced to live in Harlem, and she understood that Van Vechten, for all his wealth, was a genuine enthusiast of black talent. There are many kinds of shyness, and Bessie's violence undoubtedly sprang from hers. Van Vechten guessed as much. It was not the shyness that comes from feeling inferior; it was a shyness born out of a furious rejection of a way of life that left Bessie no room to breathe.

As gossip about Bessie's response to Van Vechten then went around Harlem, blacks delightedly incorporated her words into their own language: 'I never heard such Bessie Smith.' This remained part of their secret vocabulary, to be kept from 'Ofays'.

Bessie's lack of self-restraint became much more common among blacks paradoxically as they became more politically self-aware; the white world learnt the language of the black ghetto eagerly enough once it was used with confidence. But in Bessie's day ambitious blacks hated that language, and accepted a schoolteacher respectability which habitually looked down on the speech of the less-educated. Aspiration in Bessie's day went along with a dislike of the black idiom, black music and particularly the blues.

Nat D. Williams, a black journalist with a radio news and music history show, noted: 'You just want to be yourself and want other people to accept you for what you are. Why should I straighten my hair and put a whole lot of bleach on my skin and put on a lot of peculiar manners which are foreign to me, just to get somebody to say he's a good guy?' (quoted in McKee and Chisen-hall's *Beale Black and Blue*).

What had once seemed a barrier to acceptance has nowadays come to signify the very self-confidence that was lacking, the confidence that Bessie was asserting in her own world.

FOUR

Where did Bessie draw the courage and independence of spirit from to set up on her own? It was an age in which it was difficult for any woman to take command and, even though black women had of necessity found themselves the sole surviving prop of the family structure, there was a big gap between exercising domestic authority and nerving themselves to confronting, alone, the commercial world.

Bessie's career was bound up with the rise and collapse of the Theater Owners' Booking Association in the South, and with Columbia's 'race' records. Both grew fat in the twenties, and collapsed in the early thirties with the Depression. Both were closely bound up with a predominantly black audience, though (in the South particularly) there were many whites who loved Bessie's voice, and heard her sing in specially segregated performances.

The TOBA circuit was founded by Anselmo Barasso,

one of the brothers who owned the Palace Theater in Memphis, which was one of the biggest theatres in the South. Although ill-paid artists joked that the initials TOBA stood for 'Tough On Black Artists', the intention of the organization was to bring the black variety artists to the audience that wanted to hear them.

Bessie had been launched successfully on that circuit for more than two years before Columbia brought out her first record, 'Crazy Blues', written by Perry Bradford. But once that had registered as a hit she knew she could risk more, and from touring with a small group of other acts she was able to centre the show on herself.

Most other black women who worked as performers didn't take on the hassle of managing their own careers, let alone their own troupe as Bessie did. Even Ma Rainey depended a good deal on her husband, Will, but whatever Bessie's husband may have called himself, and whatever other support he may have given her, all show business decisions were made by Bessie.

That dominant role perhaps affected her sexuality, though unlike Ma Rainey, whose interest in her own sex was much stronger, Bessie was only touched into bisexuality when she was attracted to a particular girl, and she never lost her interest in men.

Bessie travelled with a troupe of very young and inexperienced chorus girls, glad to work for room and board and something like fifteen dollars a week. This arrangement gave Bessie enormous power over them, and she never let them forget she was the boss. She had a complex mixture of feelings for them, protective certainly but also jealous. She resented the men who wanted to make love to them. And often enough she was in love with them herself.

In some ways Bessie was a fine person to work for. She protected her girls against managers who were unfair by being prepared to put her reputation on the line. She allowed no theatre owner to object to any member of her troupe. This was true even at the end of her life, when she could no longer dictate terms.

In May 1935, for instance, when Bessie was called in as the star of a show at the Apollo because Louis Armstrong had taken a rest, she had a quarrel with the owner, Schiffman, over the chorus line. Schiffman watched one rehearsal and when the girls had left challenged Bessie about the blackness of her girls' skin. Since she was a replacement, who had no longer anything like the drawing power of Louis Armstrong by then, Bessie understood the limits of her power, but when she heard Schiffman complain that the girls were so dark they would look grey under the lights she declared she wouldn't perform without them. And she made the declaration boldly, demanding that Schiffman alter the lighting to amber. The protection of her bootlegger friend, Richard Morgan, helped her, of course; she could have hardly said otherwise that she didn't care if she went home; but it was brave, because in 1935 it meant a great deal to her to play at the Apollo.

Such gallantry won her the loyalty of her troupe all through her life.

On the other hand, she was capable of behaving with complete irresponsibility. She might leave the whole troupe behind and set off for New York in a temper. Or get so drunk that the police in some small town would have to lock her up, and the show would have to go on without her. An angry manager would dock a whole day's pay from everyone for such behaviour; and to make things more difficult, Bessie often failed to pay for hotel rooms before disappearing.

For all her travelling, Bessie never moved far away from her home ground. In those days the South spilled over into Northern cities, as hopeful blacks fled from poverty and racism. The North was Canaan; and they came out of slavery looking for the land that had been promised to them. What they usually found was a black ghetto, like Chicago's South Side; they took on flats that had to be shared on a shift basis between several families, and they listened to the latest blues in back-alley dives that offered home-made liquor. (Jazz was for whites, in cafés blacks couldn't afford.) The blues were sung with a full heart and a troubled mind, and Bessie was an incarnation of that spirit, so her audience was loyal to her; Columbia's 'race' records sold at 75 cents each in the twenties, which was an enormous slice out of a day's pay for a black worker, but Bessie's records still sold more than 20,000 copies each. And her performances were often mobbed by crowds of people whose enthusiasm for her led them to stand in queues for hours, and fight over their place.

Blues singers who travelled the same circuits as Bessie always identified with her, delightedly; Big Mama, for example, spoke of Ma Rainey, too, as being 'fat, just like I am. And she wasn't quite as tall as I am' (McKee and Chisenhall, op. cit.). But she took most pride in knowing Bessie, whom she met in Memphis at the Chicago House, enjoying her favourite food: 'I had met Bessie on the road . . . we'd sneak off in the daytime and go to those clubs and drink . . . Bessie was drinking pretty heavy then.' Big Mama clearly admired Bessie's toughness; liked her size and her willingness to fight; it was a part of the world they both inhabited. It took a great deal of courage to face up to the challenge of its continuous violence.

Coming home to Chattanooga in 1925, as a star at the Liberty Theater, an incident tested Bessie's toughness. After the last performance one night, Bessie took a few girls off to a party at the house of some old friends. She was happy to shepherd her troupe through streets which were not yet paved to a noisy house, full of people, where she could smell pig's feet and familiarly cooked greens.

Bessie and her girls were sitting at the big kitchen table eating, and drinking the home-made liquor that Bessie preferred, when an unattractive drunken man came in and wanted to dance with one of them. Bessie told him to go away and not bother them. The man didn't recognize her, and was by no means ready to give up even when Bessie rose to her feet. As he continued to challenge her, Bessie attacked him and knocked him down. She wasn't particularly dismayed. As the man fell to the ground, she went back to her food.

She didn't leave the party until a few hours later. She had no intention of letting the incident spoil her fun. But the man had bitterly resented the humiliation and he was waiting for her in the shadows with a knife. There were witnesses to the stabbing, although it was nearly four o'clock in the morning, and both police and an ambulance soon arrived. Ruby, her niece by marriage, was embellishing it a little when she spoke of the blood spurting from a wound when one of the other girls pulled the knife from Bessie's side. The doctor at the hospital suggested Bessie remain in hospital for two days, which would not be enough for a stab wound of any size; as it turned out Bessie was back on stage by two o'clock the following afternoon. A Chattanooga newspaper reported the incident as an attempted robbery, brought on by Bessie's unguarded display of costly jewellery.

In spite of the danger, Bessie felt at home in the South, particularly with her own people; and perhaps most of all with her own family, to whom she remained remarkably loyal.

She always felt responsible for her family and this included not only her brother and sisters but also their children, and involved far more than sending money to support them. She took on the role of father and mother in one, providing employment for her brothers, and setting up her sisters in suitable places to live. She trusted them with her own money, which was banked in Viola's name; and if she sometimes made use of them too (to look after her adopted child, for instance) it was by and large a one-sided relationship. If they cheated her, she shrugged the knowledge off, and if a great deal of their money went on drink, Bessie didn't care.

Her sisters shared a sloppy, unambitious life in which they simply took their share in Bessie's good fortune for granted. They neither looked up to her, nor treated her with inordinate respect. But they didn't envy her either. Bessie's second husband, Jack Gee, found their hold on Bessie infuriating, and he may have been right to be resentful on her behalf, as well as his own. But Bessie was at ease with them, and enjoyed relaxing in their company.

She loved the people she came from, as she was loyal to her own family, not out of duty but because she felt close to them. And in some of her own lyrics she wrote as if she was one of the poor herself in the tradition of wandering singers like Leadbelly or Blind Lemon, both of whom had stood on street corners and known what it was like to be unable to earn enough to buy a loaf of bread.

Poverty was a memory for Bessie once she began to sing. But she remembered her childhood, when the standard pay for blacks was a dollar a day, and blacks lived in back alleys where land was cheap, with outside toilets and garbage heaps, and in swampy areas of towns, which were often muddy and dangerously polluted. Even successful songwriters like W. C. Handy lived in a section of Memphis called Greasy Plank.

Among all this squalor, the speak-easies of Prohibition days were often glamorous and exciting places. The white rich who were adventurous enough liked to visit them. (In New York the Cotton Club attracted illicit revellers in mink and jewels.) In Memphis, mirrored walls and black seats made the Monarch Club the classiest spot in Beale Street; it was chiefly remarkable for its gambling, which attracted well-known criminals with names like Slop Crowder and Casino Harry.

FIVE

Jack Gee was the greatest love in Bessie's life, however much friends, offended by his behaviour in later years, may have wished it otherwise. And to begin with they loved one another. He was a handsome man, very big and muscular and black-skinned. He had wanted to be a policeman; when Philadelphia wouldn't accept him on their force he became a night-watchman. At the time of their first date, in 1922, Bessie was not yet making records, though she was much admired in the South. There was no reason for Jack to be intimidated by her success, or to feel the least twinge of financial opportunism. In the event, he was wounded by an unknown assailant on that first evening together; and Bessie was stirred by his physical courage and his sudden helplessness. She visited him daily at the hospital for the five weeks it took him to recover from his wound, and moved in with him when he was released.

In February 1923 Frank Walker, who was in charge

of Columbia's 'race' records, arranged Bessie's first recording through the pianist Clarence Williams. Bessie, who had been rejected by Okeh records a fortnight earlier, because her voice was 'too rough', and was still uneasy at the thought of singing into a microphone, needed a little bolstering. It was Jack who pawned his watchman's uniform and a pocket-watch to get Bessie some new clothes.

Once 'T'aint Nobody's Biz-ness If I Do' was safely on wax, Bessie was launched into a new phase of her career, though it wasn't immediately obvious. And it was at this point that Jack began to look into her business arrangements a little. It was as well he did, since, although Bessie had a show business flair which meant she was unlikely ever to be without work, she wasn't given to scrutinizing her contracts carefully. Jack can't have been illiterate, as some writers have claimed, or he would not have been able to discover that Clarence Williams, Bessie's pianist at the Columbia session, had drawn up a contract between himself and Bessie which gave him 50 per cent of her fees.

When Jack made that discovery he went round with Bessie and bullied Williams into releasing Bessie from her contract. This put 750 dollars into Bessie's pocket, which was more money than she had ever seen before; and after he talked to Frank Walker she had a new one-year contract with Columbia which guaranteed her minimum earnings of 1,500 dollars. It was Jack's first interference in Bessie's affairs, and it had gone so successfully that they left together in a state of euphoria. Neither of them observed that Frank Walker had slyly struck out the clause giving Bessie royalties on record sales, so they were still being cheated by Columbia.

Bessie's career took off in the same month that she and Jack were married; but both of them felt it was much more important they were together and having a good time. Bessie enjoyed spending money, and enjoyed having someone close to share it with her. For some time Jack went on honourably working at his job; but it kept him from touring with Bessie, and she could see no sense to it by August when she was already earning 350 dollars a week, even without royalties on record sales.

When Jack first began travelling with Bessie, it completed her happiness, and she didn't mind changing her usual habits. She had always alleviated the exhausting business of being on tour with liquor, parties and promiscuous love-making. For a while, as she travelled with her husband, all this changed, because Jack minded, and said as much. After a year of marriage, he knew she was likely to drink too much, and suspected what she might get up to if he relaxed his vigilance.

At first, Bessie tried to mollify him with presents, but she didn't enjoy having to be answerable to anyone, and she was beginning to understand what it meant to have married someone who was not part of her world. Much as she loved him, he did not bring out her gaiety, nor

47

grasp how much she needed young people who could keep up with her voracious need for excitement.

For his part, Jack needed to establish some kind of husbandly control over his wife. He was happy enough when they were crazily spending money; but he had married for love, and didn't like the feeling that everyone knew more about her doings than he did. He would have liked to take control by becoming her manager; but this she would never allow, though she often let him arrange fees for her, and she sometimes flattered him by taking his advice. When she began to disappear for more than a week at a time, he simply did not know how to deal with the situation, and could only express his anger and frustration by hitting her. Bessie minded the blows less than the constraint they imposed on her way of life.

SIX

The closest attachment Bessie formed outside her own family was to Ruby Walker, a niece of her husband Jack. Ruby had a pert, even sly, face, much prettier than her aunt's; and she hadn't been particularly impressed with Bessie on their first meeting. She looked at her aunt's size and poor clothes and felt a little superior. But when Bessie sang in Ruby's presence in Jack's mother's house on New York's 132nd Street, just before the successful recording session with Columbia in 1923, Ruby's attitude changed. She could hear Bessie's genius and she decided Bessie would be able to open a show business career for Ruby herself.

Ruby's affection, even adulation, followed, which flattered Bessie. So when Ruby begged to be allowed to go on tour, Bessie taught her a few dance steps, which Ruby learnt eagerly and easily (she had been practising for months), and arranged for Ruby to dance in the pauses while Bessie was changing her elaborate costumes.

Quite soon, as she went around night-spots with her aunt, Ruby began to admire and even envy her aunt's voracious appetite for life. She saw she couldn't hope to keep up with Bessie's drinking, and she was surprised to find that men looked to Bessie rather than herself for sexual adventure, in spite of Bessie being twenty years older. Something in the way Bessie carried herself made men forget her size and her blunt features.

Ruby's attachment coincided with Bessie's first year of success and perhaps could not have deepened without it. Ruby's early conviction that she could live as Bessie did began to fade. Bessie became the dominant person in their relationship, the one who confided, the one who chose, the one who did most of the living. Ruby tagged behind and marvelled for the most part, acknowledging that Bessie had the right to rule her own empire as she wished.

During the first year of Bessie's marriage to her uncle, Ruby learnt enough secrets to sink Bessie altogether, but she was completely loyal to her. A conspiratorial game grew up, in which Bessie took on a different personality when Jack was away. Then Ruby was at her most important to Bessie; it was also when she had most of a share in the good time. When Jack was around, Bessie had no interest in Ruby, and didn't like anyone to whisper to her about anything but the show and business, in case Jack took offence or became suspicious. Ruby was afraid of Jack and his violence; and her lifetime of covering up for Bessie was brave, as well as essential to the relationship.

Ruby's relationship with Bessie was one which had, very occasionally, to withstand rivalry between herself and her aunt. If Bessie took a fancy to one of the young male dancers in the show, she didn't expect anyone else to interfere. And when she found Ruby kissing and cuddling the handsome young Agie Pitts (a boy compared to her, as Ruby could not help observing resentfully), Bessie attacked Ruby physically to make sure she understood who could call the tune. There was never any question of it again.

Ruby was not only physically slighter; she was also less willing to be beaten up; and when Bessie attacked her in her theatre dressing room she screamed loudly enough to attract help from the police. As a result both women, and the unfortunate young dancer whose attention had wandered from Bessie, were all jailed for the night. It says something for Bessie's fondness for Ruby that she ever forgave her; but she was just the kind of woman Bessie liked. Among other qualities she possessed was one Ruby had probably not yet grasped. For Bessie to like her, she had to represent no challenge to Bessie's supremacy.

Ruby's job was to fob Jack off when he became suspicious, and cover up for Bessie when she was drinking or having a good time. Bessie began to depend on her when she got into trouble, calling her up when there were alibis to arrange, and once, when an impudent young chorus girl whom Bessie fired pressed charges for assault, needing Ruby to arrange bail.

Bessie was a large bold woman, and Ruby was a slight woman with some of the grace of a ballet dancer. Their closeness was incongruous, even though they complemented each other. And although Ruby recognized that part of the deal involved protecting Bessie from the consequences of her behaviour, she was often tired of suffering for it herself. She particularly resented the way Jack hit out at her, without considering whether she deserved it; and was perhaps all the more resentful when Bessie was making up with Jack after the quarrels. With some incredulity Ruby observed that her fat old aunt was always capable of having a better time than she was.

Bessie had the jollity of her rollicking life on the road in mind when she wrote 'Sorrowful Blues', which was recorded for Columbia in 1924. The lyric gives a humorous account of a situation she occasionally found herself in:

It's hard to love another woman's man.
It's hard to love another woman's man.
You can't get him when you want him, you got to catch
    him when you can.

When Bessie wanted Ruby's men she never had any qualms about taking them. They were often men or boys who worked for her, and there was no question of them refusing or wanting to refuse. Even towards the end of her life, when she was living happily with Richard Morgan, she was capable of stealing one, as she sings in the same song: 'I got nineteen men and I want one mo'.' These encounters weren't serious love affairs, which for Bessie meant a relationship as close as a tie of blood. They were part of her exuberant life, which she felt no need to change.

Ruby went on hoping to gain an entry to the world Bessie took for granted; but Bessie had no intention of making that easy for her. Ruby had often asked Bessie to let her see what a recording session was like; and when at last she was given a chance, in October 1925, Ruby determined to try and make the most of it. She had been practising Bessie's style of delivery, and thought she could handle it well enough to be able to record a number or two herself. She murmured as much to Frank Walker, while Bessie was singing. Whether or not she might have got her way will never be known, because Bessie, who suspected this was her intention, understood what was going on as soon as she saw Ruby talking to Frank Walker. Furiously, she made it quite clear that she would permit no such thing. But she didn't bear any malice towards Ruby for trying to make use of her, and the very same day the two women went on the town together with the 600 dollar advance Frank Walker had given Bessie.

For her part Ruby had no real grudge against her

aunt. All the excitement she had known had come to her
since she had worked with Bessie. And all the clothes she
valued had come to her in the same way. Of course, she
did not make a salary comparable to Bessie's, but Bessie's
generosity meant she often shared its advantages. It was
Bessie who gave Ruby the only fur coat she ever owned
(though, to be sure, she was the cause of its loss on one
of her escapades), and there were other presents, including expensive shoes.

It is all the more surprising to note that, when Bessie
and Jack broke up, Ruby should have decided to throw in
her lot with her uncle. Ruby's excuse, that Jack had
threatened her with violence if she refused, seems im-
plausible. It was an act of quietly desperate treachery,
activated, no doubt, by a desire to stop being nothing
more than a confidante who tagged along in the wake of
her powerful friend. It was an act which was to add yet
more bitterness to Bessie's loneliness, and would bring
Ruby little joy.

SEVEN

Bessie never carried a child of her own. That must have been by her own choice. It's hard to see a way in which she could have combined months of pregnancy with touring. Looking after a baby in itself wouldn't have been a problem, once she was earning enough money to afford a housekeeper for her husband. But she was too restless to imagine abandoning her life on the stage even for a few months. And her strong maternal drive didn't necessarily attach itself to babies. Even among children, she found her emotions aroused most by those who could walk and talk.

When she had been married two and a half years and the first signs of trouble had begun to appear between herself and Jack, Bessie decided to adopt the six-year-old child of a girl who had once worked for her, and bring him up as her own. As part of the arrangement, she brought up her sisters from Chattanooga to Philadelphia, and rented two houses for them, so that they could look after the child when she was away from home.

Bessie enjoyed the pleasures of spoiling the perky youngster. All the day-to-day care of the child was left to Viola, but Bessie found the whole experience such a delight that she changed all her plans for the summer so that she could spend it with the child. Jack found himself disliking the new arrangement. It fuelled the hostility between himself and Bessie's sisters. And he was not sanguine about Bessie taking on the permanent role of providing for the whole extended family. The new situation had cost a good deal of time and energy to set up; he knew that Bessie had spent something like 16,000 dollars on it that summer. He may also have been feeling a touch of jealousy – so Bessie seems to have suspected. To mollify him she arranged a shopping spree of his own, and they came back with a brand-new Cadillac convertible, for which Bessie had paid 5,000 dollars in cash.

After that she had to go back to work, because she was now the main bread-winner of a large family.

Bessie, an early portrait, c.1920

Ma Rainey

Ethel Waters

Ma Rainey's Georgia Jazz Band, *c.*1925

Bessie, centre front, at the Paradise in Atlantic City with fellow performers and Charlie Johnson's orchestra, c.1920

Bessie and Jack Gee soon after their wedding in 1923

Catalogue for Columbia's 'race' records, 1928

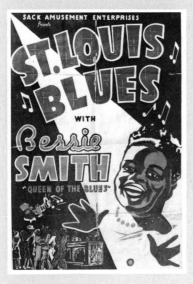

Film poster for *St Louis Blues*, 1929

Still from *St Louis Blues:* Bessie with Jimmie Mordecai as her lover

Bessie on stage, *c.*1929

Bessie with Richard Morgan, shortly before the fatal car accident

Bessie, 'Queen of the Blues', 1936

EIGHT

Jack was stronger than Bessie, and she respected him most when he challenged her physically.

His role, as he accompanied her on her travels, was not so different from his earlier job as night-watchman and guard. Bessie kept the money she earned on tour in a safe on the train. Jack travelled with a loaded gun, and watched when the safe was opened to put money away, or take money out on pay-day.

The closest Bessie came to living an ordinary domestic life was in Philadelphia in the autumn of 1925, when she enjoyed a rest after an enormously successful year. She let herself relax and live sloppily, not bothering to dress up even when she went out to a neighbour's home. And Jack was happy to have her live as she liked. But it was a brief idyll. When Bessie went back to work the marriage began to shudder under the strain.

By this time Jack knew very well that Bessie was deceiving him whenever she could, and he became less concerned with preventing the infidelity than with catching her out and punishing her. Bessie knew as much and was afraid of him, because he hit her so hard when they fought. And Ruby, too, wondered if one day he might not actually kill her. The violence stepped up, and even though Bessie continued to think of him as her man she also continued to drink and had no intention of living with him faithfully.

It was not surprising that Jack drew away from her. He had never enjoyed drinking as Bessie did. He no longer enjoyed sitting in the audience watching her perform; and his role as moral policeman to the troupe was becoming tedious. And as he began to look for new ways to define himself, he began to realize that money, rather than love, was what bound him to Bessie.

Bessie was not so innocent as to be unaware of the shift in his attention. But she could not see how to change her way of life. So they were on a collision course.

Jack did what Bessie asked when there were chores to be done, as he had when all Bessie's relations had to be moved up from Chattanooga to Philadelphia, but he began to resent the way Bessie made use of him. Even more he objected to Bessie's family treating him as a paid dependant and taking Bessie's generosity for granted. He could see that Bessie's sisters had no intention of doing any work again. And the fact that he was doing little work himself hardly helped to sustain him.

By sending her money to Viola, rather than Jack, to bank, Bessie was really doing little more than asserting the primacy of the family bond. It was entirely fortuitous that success and her marriage to Jack together produced a new situation. (In Bessie's brief earlier marriage there had been no money to complicate her relationships, and so there were no difficulties between husband and family.) Jack was deeply suspicious of Viola in any case; now he had the humiliation of having to ask her for any money he needed. When he stayed obediently at home it was Viola who drew from the bank whatever Bessie said he could have. There was no generosity that could overcome his feeling that she trusted him less than Viola and kept tighter rein on him than on her sisters.

It was inevitable that he himself should begin to snatch at love elsewhere. Bessie discovered as much one night in late 1926, when she returned from New York. Jack was supposed to be waiting for her in the train with the *Harlem Frolics* troupe in Ozark, Alabama. This time there was no happy reunion. A chorus girl told Bessie that Jack had been having an affair with one of the other girls. Bessie was furious, and like an empress of old, took out her fury first on the messenger, throwing her with all her clothes right off the train, before she set off to look for Jack up and down the car. She did not find Jack there, but she did find his gun, and when he did appear, walking down the track, she fired it at him. He was not a physical coward, and he went on coming towards the train even as she herself. The gesture had affected Bessie deeply but now she seemed almost indifferent to Lillian's departure.

She had been relatively sober since the shooting incident, but now that Lillian had gone there was nothing to distract her from her old ways of having a good time. These included visiting the notorious 'buffet flats' in Detroit, which put on various kinds of erotic shows, with exhibitions of male homosexuality and amazing sexual turns involving Coca Cola bottles and lighted cigarettes. And of course she drank heavily.

The troupe was staying in a boarding-house in the town, and on their last night in Detroit were all gathered in Bessie's room to celebrate the success of their week there. The party was in full swing, and several members of the troupe had either passed out or gone to bed, including Ruby. Bessie and a new young girl, Marie, had just made their way to bed together when Jack appeared, banging doors and demanding to know where his wife was. Someone managed to mislead him, and soon the terrified women were gathering all their clothes together and setting off for the railroad car as fast as they could.

It was the first of many similar exploits. Bessie knew her behaviour was enraging Jack dangerously, but she was too obstinate to change it. Probably Jack found her relations with women a much more serious rejection than he would have found a love affair with someone of his own sex. Bessie, on the other hand, must have thought of these encounters as a part of life on the road which was not his business. None the less, she could not but have been aware that she was goading him like a mad bull. Whenever he came into her dressing-room, he hit out at everyone and threatened worse, and Bessie had to run away, sometimes leaving the show altogether and once being forced to leave a favourite fur coat behind and make her escape in pyjamas.

Bessie did not decide that there was nothing in her relationship to save. About this time she bought her sister Viola a restaurant in South Street, Philadelphia, with the hope of making her financially independent. This was something she organized with Jack's old resentment very much in mind.

Jack too had a confusion of ambivalent emotions which he could not deal with. Certainly Bessie's behaviour hurt him. And about the time she arranged for Viola to start life as a restaurant owner, Jack had the first of many nervous breakdowns, which took him to Hot Springs in Alabama.

Not everyone believes in the genuineness of these attacks, but the particular form of the pretence (if pretence it was, which I doubt) is psychologically significant in itself. Jack made himself seem helpless, as he had been in the first five weeks of their relationship, and this brought Bessie to his side at once with loving concern. They made up their quarrels, and Bessie stayed at his side to nurse him and give him what he wanted.

Back on the road, though, it was a different and more difficult relationship, and there was no way in which Bessie could earn the income she wanted without touring, even if she had been prepared to change her life to settle down with Jack. And for all his enjoyment of her attention in Hot Springs it is at least possible that he would not have welcomed her full-time presence without the wealth she brought with her. Of course, if Columbia had paid her royalties her choices would have been different, as they would if her personality had made it possible for her to find a base in a long-playing show in New York. Ethel Waters was not the only one of her fellow blues singers to find that that was a possible move. But Bessie never aimed at it. She liked her way of life.

She kept on drinking heavily, although she had to keep it from Jack, because if he caught her drinking he still beat her up; their quarrels were now followed by longer separations. The pattern was repeated several times in 1929, and Bessie took to announcing that the marriage was completely over, but as there were re-conciliations after every quarrel her friends took less and less notice.

Bessie was exasperated by her own behaviour, and was increasingly angry at what she felt was a weakness. How could someone as independent as she had always been find herself in a relationship where she was afraid to do what she wanted? The trouble was that she still loved Jack, for all her outrageous refusal to behave as he wanted, and she couldn't break away from him, however violent he became.

Her bewilderment found expression in her own blues lyric, 'Please Help Me Get Him Off My Mind', which expresses her impatience with the way she was living:

I cried and worried, all night I laid and groaned,
I cried and worried, all night I laid and groaned,
I used to weigh two hundred, now I'm down to skin and
    bone.
It's all about a man, who always kicks and dogs me
    aroun',
It's all about a man, who always kicks and dogs me
    aroun',
And when I try to kill him, that's when my love for him
    comes down.
I've come to see you, gypsy, beggin' on my bended knee,
I've come to see you, gypsy, beggin' on my bended knee,
That man put somethin' on me; oh, take it off of me
    please.

Bessie had always let Jack put the prefix 'Jack Gee presents' on all her own road-shows, however little hand he had in their organization. He brought out a gentleness in her. And she knew he needed self-respect. So, for all their fighting, she was willing to give Jack 3,000 dollars to set up the production of a new show which was to be called *Steamboat Days*. She understood his male vulnerability, and the offer of money was an attempt both to bolster him and to save their marriage. She continued to need that marriage, and Jack, much as she might have preferred not to. She needed his love, or the illusion of it. He knew as much, and took advantage of it treacherously, by taking some of the money he had been given to finance *Steamboat Days* to set up another show for a star whose singing talent was small, but who had the light, perky-featured good looks that Bessie found enraging.

Jack's sexual relationship with Gertrude Saunders was not new, and he may have hoped to conceal his financial involvement. But Gertie Saunders's tour, and Jack's support of it, were inevitably reported in the press. Bessie read of them while she was on tour herself in Cincinnati.

For all her public calm as she left her friends after reading that newspaper item, what Bessie felt was not so much anger as pain. In her dressing-room, alone with Ruby, she broke down and cried. It was the first time Ruby had ever seen her weep. 'Ruby, I'm *hurting*,' she said, 'I'm *hurting*' (quoted in Chris Albertson's *Bessie*).

It took all her courage to make herself go on-stage. She said. 'Ruby, fix my feathers.' And although she went on, the performance did not ease her; and perhaps she was not altogether cured ever again. The bitterness entered her face, and could be seen there years later. Frank Walker put that down to her disappointment at the way her career turned in the thirties; but he was mistaken. It was the bitterness of discovering that the most familiar story of the blues was after all her own.

As soon as the show ended, Bessie went straight out into the street with Ruby to look for a cab, and when she found one asked it to take them all the way to Columbus, Ohio, where Gertrude Saunders's new show was playing. She arrived at about two o'clock in the morning, calm by then, and more furious than tearful. She seems to have presented Jack with some kind of ultimatum, as well as beating him angrily, because Jack behaved as if he had made a decision to abandon Gertie and return to Bessie. This remained his claim throughout the last half of his life; yet the game was over. Bessie could no longer play it.

She tried for a few days. She drank deeply; and she still wanted to patch things up. Her temper and her pride prevented it. Before her engagement in Cincinnati was over, she packed up and left. The troupe was thrown into disarray by this and it was Jack's idea to save the show by trying Ruby out as a substitute. He may have been clever enough to realize that that would infuriate Bessie more than anything else, and, sure enough, it brought back an angry Bessie in protest. His gamble hardly paid off, however, since Bessie not only ordered Ruby off the stage, but ordered Jack out of her life. Something had died between them, and she knew she would have to make the break. The pain of that decision did not heal quickly.

In no ordinary sense was Bessie dependent on Jack, but it turned out to be very difficult for her to bear life without him. Her rage dwindled into loneliness and unhappiness. She could have lived as riotously as she wanted now, but the heart seemed to have gone out of such frivolity. When she went to bed she couldn't sleep.

The grief she felt can be heard in May 1929 not so much as sorrow but as knowledge, as Bessie recorded 'Nobody Knows You When You're Down and Out'.

This is the song which has attached itself most closely to her name, the song in which her cynicism is at its most poignant, her voice at its most deceptively relaxed. The song assumes a world which has no interest in losers. It is not a song that she wrote herself, but she sings the words as if they came straight out of her own pain. The generous spirit which takes friends out to drink when she has money and finds no one when it is gone could be her own; and though she was not down and out, she was certainly brought low.

Anyone who doubts Bessie's artistry should listen to that recording. (And it is artistry, and not sincerity in a crude sense; she was able to record an exuberant version of 'I Got What It Takes, But It Breaks My Heart to Give It Away' in the same session.)

Once I lived the life of a millionaire
Spending all my money, I didn't care;
I carried my friends out for a good time,
Buyin' bootleg liquor, champagne and wine.

When I began to fall so low,
I didn't have a friend and no place to go,

So, if I ever get my hands on a dollar again,
I'm going to hang on to it 'til them eagles grin.

Nobody knows you when you're down and out.
In my pocket, not one penny, and my friends, I haven't
    any;
But if I ever get on my feet again, then I'll meet those
    long-lost friends;
It's mighty strange, without a doubt,
Nobody knows you when you're down and out.

She hardly seems to be working at all; and yet we are moved. When she comes to repeat the song after the instrumental chorus, her voice sings some of the lines as a long-drawn-out *Hmmmm*, which is infinitely touching; while a residual jauntiness in 'if I ever get on my feet again' carries the assurance that she has not given up altogether. Jack's betrayal went deep, because he had come to represent a stability and a sweetness she feared she would never find again. It wasn't simply that she judged herself by different rules to him (though she clearly did); her activities did not destroy her dependency upon him or her way of thinking about him. His cheating her out of money to impress a rival went to the very heart of their relationship.

NINE

Some idea of how Bessie looked and moved in that disastrous year of 1929 can be found in a short film based on W. C. Handy's 'St Louis Blues'. Dressed in a printed gown with a low-slung waist, Bessie stands with one arm on her hip, several stone heavier than her rival. She has a handsome, solidly modelled face; her rival is closer to the prevailing fashion.

The story of the film comes alarmingly close to Bessie's own situation. The woman she plays is betrayed by a man she is keeping, who prefers someone with neater features and a slimmer build. And the woman she plays is also called Bessie.

One of the reasons W. C. Handy chose her for the part was Bessie's magnificent version of his song 'St Louis Blues', on which the whole film turns. He needed Bessie's voice because of its strength, which could make itself heard above the orchestra and choir he planned as background. Under a pleated cap that hugged her head, her face is tender and expressive in close-up. It is not a particularly attractive get-up, but Bessie's mouth is so mobile and feeling, and her eyes crackle with such animation that it is easy to see why she attracted so much male attention.

The film was shot on Long Island, but the action is supposed to take place in a boarding-house in Memphis. The central character steps over a group of men playing dice, and makes her way back to her room, where she finds her boyfriend with a young rival. Bessie throws the girl out, but is knocked to the floor by her unfaithful boyfriend and begins to sing 'St Louis Blues', with a bottle in her hand.

The stereotypes of film presentation of black life are all there: gambling, drinking and immorality. But the film is nevertheless remarkable. It is the only footage we have of Bessie's singing and it gives us a chance to see the animation in a face that often looks impassive on still photographs. The scene changes to a bar, where Bessie continues her song over a drink, and there is a brief shot of the Fletcher Henderson Band as they (and a large choir) join in. When her boyfriend returns and dances with her Bessie's radiance lights her whole face; but he has only returned in order to slip the last of her money from the top of her stocking, and as he struts out she is left singing the blues, after a brief intimation of possible happiness.

Bessie would not have found the role of a strong

woman keeping her parasitic man unfamiliar even if she had not come to have that relationship with Jack; it was one of the commonest relationships that the ghetto set up. Women found employment more easily than men in the South, by no means necessarily through immorality. Domestic work was usually open when all hope of other employment failed. Hence songs like Leadbelly's, which recalls ruefully how the departure of his meal-ticket woman has left him walking about in an unaccustomed search for work.

TEN

Whatever Jack did for the rest of his life he could never get free of his Empress, or fail to understand that his relationship with her was the thing which most interested people about him. This was difficult for him, but it doesn't excuse his behaviour in the years after he and Bessie separated. By far the cruellest of his acts was his trying to get back at Bessie through her adopted son, Jack Gee, Jun. The fact that the child carried his name did not mean that Jack had any affection for him, and it's hard to see how Jack's intention could have been anything other than simple vengeance.

It is a strange story. Jack arrived at Bessie's house when she wasn't there, and told his ten-year-old son to get in the car. Then he drove him to the Society of Prevention of Cruelty to Children, where he reported that the child was allowed to stay out all night and refused to go to school. There was some truth in the second statement and (though the boy denied it) there could well have been truth in the first without it being a sufficient justification for such behaviour.

Bessie was out of her mind with worry and fury; and the SPCC decided that there was a *prima facie* case. Luckily, when the case came to court, the judges decided that the child should be returned to his mother's custody, with only one condition: that he should remain with Viola in Philadelphia.

It was partly Jack Jun.'s fault that the next disaster occurred. Much as he loved Bessie, he did not find his life in Philadelphia particularly exciting in her absence. And his decision to try and make his way back to New York at the end of a fortnight sealed his fate. However a black child of ten aroused the attention of the relevant authorities, Jack Jun. did so. And he was caught, in Newark, New Jersey, taken into care and released into his father's control. It is at this point that Jack's malice is clearest. He didn't want the child living with him, and Gertie Saunders hated the child, who was sent downstairs to live in the basement. No attempt was made to welcome him, or even feed him; and it was Gertie's brother (who also lived in the basement) who gave the boy money to go out and buy food. The boy used the opportunity to try and escape; and in a short time he wound up in the hands of the SPCC again. They decided he was clearly in need of care and protection and sent him away for it to Valhalla, in New York State.

Bessie didn't know where he was; and the boy did not

get in touch with her by letter for several days. Jack was told what had happened to the boy, but he had no desire to ease Bessie's anxiety, and she seems to have given up hope of getting the child back. She now hated Jack with all the passion she'd once put into loving him, and her loneliness was so painful that many days she just sat, staring into space, completely broken. Everything she loved had been taken from her, and she didn't even try to put things right.

Altogether, 1929 was an unlucky year for Bessie. When Maceo Pickard (who had written 'Sweet Georgia Brown') offered her the chance to star in a Broadway show, she was glad enough of the lift. She was well aware of the changes in the entertainment world which were going to send vaudeville out of business. But there was only a fortnight for rehearsal, the story line of *Pansy* dealt with college activities, and Pickard was not an experienced producer. Bessie accepted the chance, and it was not her fault that the opportunity did her career more harm than good. She was far from finished as far as recording was concerned. Indeed, she made one of her most remarkable records during the week of the show's brief run. *Pansy* attracted appalling reviews, even though critics observed Bessie's presence with respect, and it is unsurprising that the show closed after only three days.

If Bessie's story takes a turn for the better just before the end, it is entirely because of the love and loyalty of

Richard Morgan. He had admired her since her earliest appearances in Birmingham, Alabama, and when he had successfully set himself up as a bootlegger on Chicago's South Side he had an opportunity to entertain her, along with Louis Armstrong and Jelly Roll Morton, at the kind of party she loved. Even then he clearly had a very particular admiration for her, which he showed by making sure everyone stopped laughing and talking before she started to sing, a courtesy he paid none of the other brilliant entertainers who came to his house.

In 1930, when the Wall Street Crash had worked its way down to the TOBA circuit, and Bessie's record sales had dipped to an all-time low, she set off on a tour which led her through Chicago. And there Richard Morgan showed himself still warm and affectionate and eager to set up a new relationship after breaking up with his common-law wife, Lucy. So the worst effects of the Depression never reached Bessie, because probably the only business that wasn't destroyed in those bleak years was the bootlegger's, and Morgan prospered.

She was never obsessively in love with him as she had been with Jack; but they were good friends, tolerant of one another, and Morgan treated her well. He did not object to her drinking, and wasn't shocked at her undisciplined behaviour. His patience sustained her for the rest of her life.

Richard Morgan was Lionel Hampton's uncle, and Hampton remembers vividly both the early parties in

Chicago and his devotion to Bessie in the years they were together. 'I don't believe there was anything he wouldn't do for her' (Albertson, op. cit.).

If we do not have such a good picture of Richard Morgan as we do of Jack Gee it is partly because he was a much quieter man. Even when he was drunk he remained even-tempered and in control. We can guess something of his life, which ought not to be sentimentalized. No one could be a gangster in Chicago in the twenties with clean hands, and no one could run a successful bootlegging business without the support of a gang.

Bessie, who had spent years on the barrel-house circuits, was not bothered by that. Night-life flourished in the underworld and the world did not frighten her. For the first time in her life she was protected as well as loved, and the pain of Jack's betrayal began to heal. She did not behave particularly well in return; she still went off drinking wildly when she was away from home; and Richard had to bail her out of jails more than once because she had got into a fight; but he seems to have loved her enough to accept everything she did.

Bessie was lucky to find such love. In staying with Richard, she cheated the commonest experience of fellow singers who had settled for a series of husbands; nearly all experienced deep loneliness when they cut themselves free. And Bessie was not to be lonely again.

Richard Morgan's help was a cushion for Bessie through the years when the vaudeville theatres closed up all over America, and the slump killed the record companies. It was, nevertheless, in the thirties that Bessie paid most for her earlier refusal of the white world.

She saw the way things were going in the entertainment business. But by 1930 it was already too late. Records were becoming a luxury few could afford; and the TOBA organization folded up completely in the summer of that year. Hollywood and the Broadway stage had begun to show signs of the Depression themselves, and were no longer looking for talent, let alone black talent from an earlier period.

Ethel Waters missed out on some of the worst of the Depression by being in Paris; and when she returned she was able to draw on an audience who were not yet devastated by the economic climate. Her first show, *Blackbirds*, flopped, but she was able to negotiate a good contract with Lew Leslie for *Rhapsody in Black*, on Broadway, which brought her in over 2,000 dollars a week. It was a show that succeeded admirably at the box-office, and Ethel benefited because she had arranged for a percentage of the take. Ethel went on receiving good money and acclaim in the very years Bessie was hustling from town to town on the old circuits in the South. She was honoured with a special 'Ethel Waters Night' at the Cotton Club; and accepted invitations to perform for Al Jolson with Fred and Adele Astaire. When Bessie was at the height of her fame the obstinate rejection of a whole style of life looked admirable. But as she approached forty her determination to do everything in her own way was showing its limitations.

It is not necessary to avoid the speculation; did the defiant choice really arise from wholly different values? It seems to spring more from a lack of worldliness; which isn't a virtue. The instinct to compromise does not bring immortality of course, but Bessie might well have preferred some of the temporal pleasures.

Bessie was far from down and out. She could still earn five to seven hundred dollars a week, and from Alabama to Texas she could still fill a theatre. But the bread-lines were lengthening, and theatres were closing, and it was becoming clear to everyone that the Depression was not going to lift easily.

She recorded 'Black Mountain Blues' for Columbia in July 1930, and it is one of her most magnificent performances; but Columbia was on the verge of bankruptcy, and when the record was released in October they only pressed 2,095 copies.

There was a certain irony in the title of Bessie's new show: *Broadway Revue*. Bessie travelled a long way from Broadway with it in 1931. The audiences were still enthusiastic; and sometimes she was held over for another week. But the long-term outlook for her work was poor, and she knew it. Her voice was as strong as ever, but her chances of reaching people with it were diminishing, and in November 1931, when she went to record two sides for Columbia, Frank Walker had to tell her that Columbia would not be taking up her option. In the nine years Bessie had been with Columbia she had been paid only a fraction of what her records had earned them, and she still had no royalty agreement.

When she appeared at the Grand, in Chicago, in February 1932, her success led a reviewer from Pittsburgh to write: 'Bessie Smith, herself, is back in town at the Grand theater. And we don't mean maybe. She's singing "Please Don't Talk About Me When I'm Gone" and "Safety Woman Looking For a Safety Man". Bessie has a real humane personality . . .'

This delighted witness of Bessie's success was either unaware that Bessie only earned 200 dollars for her week in Chicago, or thought she would benefit more from his enthusiasm if she seemed not to be losing her hold. Actually, the packed audience may have been there not to see Bessie but the film *Possessed* with Clark Gable and Joan Crawford, stars of the new era who were displacing variety acts all over the country, and with whom Bessie had perforce to share the bill.

When Bessie could see a large audience out front, she gave them her best, and they loved her. Art Hodes, the pianist, in a article in *Jazz Record*, recalled one of her appearances in Chicago, resplendent in a shimmering white evening-gown, and declared that she completely dominated the stage as she always did: 'There's no explainin' her singing, her voice. She don't need a mike; she don't use one . . . As she sings she moves slowly round the stage. Her head, sort of bowed. From where I'm sittin' I'm not sure whether she even has her eyes open. On and on, number after number, the same hush, the great performance, the deafening applause.'

The trouble lay not so much in Bessie's performance, nor in her effect on an audience when she had one. Bessie had never had an agent or a manager to arrange theatre appearances for her, but that old self-reliance was now beginning to look something of a mistake. The TOBA circuit had gone for ever and in its absence it was easier to see what a helpful function it had had. Without any supporting network, offers began to come in more and more rarely, and without Richard Morgan Bessie might well have been reduced to finding other work to keep her going. But though her spirits were lowered by her falling earnings, she was well provided for. Sometimes (for instance, in October 1933) she spent a whole month at home with him in Philadelphia.

The downward momentum of her career must have looked unstoppable, although there were signs of an alleviation of the Depression. Roosevelt was in the White House, and people hoped some good would come of that. And Bessie was asked to make records again, for Okeh, whose offices, like Columbia's, were now at 55 Fifth Avenue. Bessie's producer was John Hammond, but she made all the decisions about her choice of tunes for the recording session. There was a formidably talented group of musicians accompanying her, many of them stars of the new era of swing, including Jack Teagarden on trombone and Benny Goodman (brought in from a neighbouring studio) on clarinet. Bessie's voice is at her rowdiest and most confident in 'Gimme a Pigfoot', and musically she shows a new kind of flexibility. Listening to her then it seems possible she could have moved into the era of the big bands. Her voice was certainly powerful enough, and she understood musically what she needed to do.

Jack Jun. remained one of the most important people in Bessie's life, though she didn't have much hope of getting him out of the clutches of the homes that looked after him. It was the child's memory of Bessie's love that made him continue writing to her long after she had given up trying. He was pretty ingenious at finding addresses to make contact with her, for someone who was regarded as more or less uneducable. He wrote to Frank Walker at Columbia; and pursued her even though she had moved houses and wrote no letter to him.

All through 1930 and 1931 Jack Jun. was in a home first in Easton, Maryland, then in St Martin's, but in November 1932 he was discharged into the care of his father. And when he wrote from New York how much he wanted to be with her, Bessie had no hesitation in taking action, which she knew had to be brutally decisive, because Jack was likely to be violent. She arrived with Richard Morgan, her sister-in-law Maud's brother and her own brother Teejay, to make a powerful group he would have to yield to. Jack saw as much, and let the boy go without fuss.

Then Bessie was happy for the first time since her marriage had collapsed in 1929, even if Jack Jun. did not altogether settle down as she wanted. He found it difficult to settle in any place, though he loved Bessie more than anyone, and she spoiled him whatever he did; it was soon clear that he had no interest at all in school or in making something of himself. He was much more interested in having a good time, as Bessie had been, but he had none of her show business talent to help him. Bessie, who rapidly resorted to her fists in all her relationships, hit her son hard once when he admitted how much he hated his schooling. It was the only time she hit him, and then it was out of fear as much as disappointment. She was frightened that the truancy officer might take the child away from her again. Whatever he did, she went on giving him as much money as he wanted even though she was dependent on Morgan after she had stopped earning a big salary.

She tried to bribe him with clothes and the offer of a car to work hard for the grades that would make it possible for him to study law; but Jack had no inclination in that direction. His friends weren't studious; and he had a good deal of experience of life on the other side of the law from his days in homes. He often disappeared for days at a time, but Bessie of course was often away herself and in any case wasn't given to worrying.

That she made no provision for him in her will shows how far away she was from thinking of dying in the years which preceded her death. She was, in spite of her maternal anxiety, proud of her son, and happy to have him with her.

It had taken Bessie a long while to recover from the pain of losing her husband Jack, and she never stopped hating Gertie Saunders. Friends were so aware of this that they were afraid to mention their names, much less any occasion when they might have seen Jack and Gertie together. But Jack remained with Gertie for some time, even though Gertie always found Bessie's jealousy a threat, and looked down on Jack Gee as too black and too ignorant.

Gertie's own charm was one of the key factors in arousing Bessie's fury. All the humiliations she had suffered at the hands of producers like Irvin C. Miller at the start of her career must have returned as she brooded. To lose Jack to a girl who thought herself better because of her manners and the lack of pigment in her skin was intolerable. For someone as ready to use violence as Bessie was, Gertie's snobbery was a powerful impulse to murder, and many friends were afraid of a physical encounter that could prove fatal.

Gertie must have been afraid of that, too. She had an altogether slighter build, and Jack could hardly guard her all the time. On one occasion not long after the split, when both Gertie and Bessie were on the road, they met in a small town in the Midwest. A bad flood had made it difficult for Gertie's show to leave, and as Bessie and her troupe began to make their way through the muddy streets to the hotel, Bessie suddenly saw Gertie and Jack ahead of her and determined to take vengeance. For all his strength, Jack couldn't prevent Bessie throwing Gertie down in the mud, tearing her hair and beating her face viciously. All the time she did so she uttered threats of even worse; and it is surprising that Gertie recovered well enough to continue her tour.

The two women had another encounter, a few years later, in Harlem. While he was still with Bessie, Jack had opened a barber's store opposite the Lafayette Theater, with the idea of salting some money away; and later Gertie bought the candy and tobacco store next door to his as show business began to look bleak. Bessie had taken an apartment on West 133rd Street. She had been told that Jack had given some of her jewellery to Gertie, and she called one day to collect it.

All stories agree that Bessie was given a pawn ticket which in the upshot only yielded cheap jewels. According to Gertie, there was no fight, even though Bessie was drunk; according to others, Bessie beat the girl unconscious. It is hard to believe that Bessie was simply talked out of her rage by Gertie's calm demeanour, particularly as she was drunk at the time. More likely, Gertie, who felt that fights were degrading, lied about this one.

ELEVEN

Death was waiting for Bessie on Route 61 south of Memphis at three o'clock on a Sunday morning, in the form of a National Biscuit Company truck parked without lights at the roadside. Bessie approached in her old wooden-topped Packard, with Richard Morgan at the wheel. Her arm rested on the side of the car as it splintered against the truck's tail-gate. The truck-driver rapidly drove off into the darkness, and Bessie never regained consciousness, though she did not die for another eight and a half hours.

The sequence of events leading up to her death remains far from easy to straighten out. The story is best known now through Edward Albee's play *The Death of Bessie Smith*; and even at the time she was treated as a martyr to Southern racism. The thought of her death as an unknown black woman refused treatment interested journalists more than her life had done. In her dying she earned more column inches in the white press than she ever had in her life.

The only eye-witness to set out an account of the events was the doctor who attended her at the wayside; and his account differs on many points from the earliest versions that appeared in the press. No reporter ever asked Richard Morgan (who was hurt, but still able to flag down the doctor's car) what had happened, though he did tell his story to Bessie's family; and a version of it, in the memory of Bessie's son, Jack Gee, Jun., is presented in an interview with *Afro-American* about five years after Bessie's death.

The original article to set off the legend of Bessie dying because she was turned away by a white hospital was written by the man who had organized Bessie's last recording session with Okeh. John Hammond's article, which appeared in *Downbeat* (and which probably provided the trigger for Albee's play nearly a quarter of a century later), carried the inflammatory headline: 'DID BESSIE SMITH BLEED TO DEATH WHILE WAITING FOR MEDICAL AID?' The place, the parked truck and the delay before an ambulance arrived agree with other accounts. But the key assertion (for which Hammond had no evidence) was explicit, however qualified in his next paragraph: 'When finally she did arrive at the hospital she was refused treatment because of her color, and bled to death while waiting for attention.'

The only hospital records that exist are those of the G. T. Thomas Hospital for blacks in Clarksdale, Mississippi, where Bessie died after admission. It might be argued that the white hospital which turned Bessie away would be hardly likely to have kept a record of the incident, but the black hospital staff were sufficiently indignant at Hammond's story to write in to *Downbeat* saying that Bessie had died in their ward after being brought directly from the roadside. It is barely possible that they did so because they were alarmed by the tone of Hammond's piece – 'Of the particular city of Memphis I am prepared to believe almost anything' – but against that possibility must be set the sheer improbability of an ambulance driver, still less a black ambulance driver, taking *any* black person to a white hospital in the thirties.

The doctor who attended to Bessie at the roadside gave an interview to *Esquire* in 1969 and to Chris Albertson for his magnificent book *Bessie*. Early on Sunday morning, 26 September 1937, Dr Smith and a companion left Memphis on Route 61 to go fishing, and about seventy miles south of the city they saw the wreck of a big car lying across the road. He claims to have also seen the body of a woman in the road, a man waving at him and the red tail-lights disappearing. If this were true, he must have arrived only minutes after the accident. The most important of Dr Smith's observations, however, concern the nature of Bessie's injuries, and the circumstances leading up to her being taken to the hospital.

Dr Smith suggested that at the moment of impact Bessie was probably asleep with her arm out of the car, or perhaps with only her elbow protruding. All the bones round the elbow were completely shattered and there was a total circumferential interruption of soft tissues above the elbow; yet in spite of her forearm having been torn loose from her upper arm, the two major vessels, the artery and the nerve were intact. 'What it boils down to is that the hemorrhage from the arm did not cause death.'

He registered the horrible mess of blood in the road, but gave his categorical opinion that, if the severed arm had been her only injury, she would have survived. The cause of death, he decided, must lie in the severe injuries to her entire right side. His examination showed that all the ribs on her right side were crushed, and he guessed at an internal haemorrhage as well as head injuries.

That would fit in with the G. T. Thomas Hospital's report that Bessie died of 'Shock' and 'Possible internal injuries', as well as the compound fracture of her arm.

Dr Smith's companion is said to have summoned an ambulance while Dr Smith was tending Bessie – on foot, I assume, since Dr Smith's car continued to stand in the road. Dr Smith makes mention (but says little further) of another car which approached and drove straight into the back of his own while he was tending Bessie. In that second car was a white couple: a young lady, unhurt but scared to death, and a man who received chest injuries from his steering-wheel. In the event, two ambulances arrived on the scene almost at the same time (one called unexpectedly by the National Biscuit Company truck-driver) so any greater urgency felt in getting the white couple sent off to the hospital did not affect Bessie's chances.

Nevertheless, there are some unaccountable delays. Dr Smith emphatically rebuts the story of Bessie being taken to a white hospital first: 'Bessie Smith would *not* have gone to a white hospital, you can forget that . . .' He has no evidence on the point, but it's useful to know that the two hospitals were only a mile apart. Whatever the delay was, it was hardly caused by a one-mile diversion.

Bessie did not die until eleven-thirty the same morning. Dr Smith put his arrival at ten minutes after the accident, and if he really saw the lights of the truck it might possibly have been even less, and guesses that another fifteen went by before the ambulance arrived. If that was the distance and time Dr Smith believed himself to be away from the hospital, it is hard to explain why Bessie received no treatment for over seven hours (the accident having taken place around 3:00 a.m.). When did the ambulances arrive?

Dr Smith must have his times wildly wrong. Perhaps he wished to forget that he did not choose to take Bessie to hospital himself. According to Jack Gee, Jun., who heard the story from Richard Morgan before he died, it was Richard who walked into Clarksdale (ten miles away) to get an ambulance. A ten-mile walk when there was a car available would help to account for the delay in treatment; Richard would hardly have left Bessie until the doctor had completed his examination, so there was no medical reason for the doctor not to have driven for help. In Richard Morgan's account there is quite a crowd of spectators; Dr Smith's story is filled with night-time country noises, which he describes with surprising lyricism. Perhaps he wanted to forget the presence of other people. Morgan suggests that one of those spectators asked Dr Smith why he didn't take Bessie into Clarksdale himself and Dr Smith is said to have replied that it would make his car too bloody. Whether or not he actually said any such thing, the fact remains that he did not take Bessie back to the hospital, and that he nowhere excuses this by saying it would damage Bessie.

Again, according to Jack Gee, Jun., Richard Morgan remembered the injured white couple and claims that, when he came back with the ambulance, someone in the crowd said: 'Let's see what's the matter with the white woman first.' If Dr Smith permitted that, and the white woman was sent back to Clarksdale in spite of Richard Morgan's protests, it may not go very far towards explaining the delay; but since the arrival of the second ambulance, sent by the guilty truck-driver, could hardly have been expected by Dr Smith, it begins to suggest a good deal about Dr Smith's attitude to Bessie. Jack Gee, Jun.'s memory was articulated much earlier than Dr Smith's; and Dr Smith's account does not substantially correct his except, rather dubiously, on the question of who went for the ambulance.

This is hardly a matter Richard would be likely to forget, and if we had his direct evidence on the matter I should be inclined to accept it. But of course we only have his opinion second-hand. If we do accept Jack Gee, Jun.'s version as authentic, it suggests that Dr Smith's more or less unconscious racism contributed to the delay in getting Bessie to the hospital. It does not establish that the delay was decisive. And in the mess of conflicting detail we are not likely to get much closer to the facts.

inside her all the time and she was just bound to find it.'
He knew from his early days working with Bessie in *How
Come* (which Bessie played in 1923) how Bessie's troubled
spirit would not let her rest. It was almost chemical, a
mood that took her over, so that she could never live
peacefully. It must have been in the grip of that mood
that she shouted so rudely at the boss of *How Come* that
he replaced her with Alberta Hunter.

When Bessie gave a rare interview to the *Chicago
Defender*, on 29 March 1937, she named the chief influences on her music as Cora Fisher and W. C. Handy.
It is a surprising choice. Of course this may be an in-
vention of the journalist: the date of her birth is falsi-
fied, and the journalist speaks of Bessie having given her
first week's wages to her mother when the poor woman
was dead before Bessie had earned any. W. C. Handy
was not himself a powerful musician though he was
responsible for putting out numerous blues songs, and
invented many of them. Pianists like Jelly Roll Morton
found him irritatingly square, and he certainly included
a large number of strings in his own band. For Bessie,
though, he was the man who had not only written 'St
Louis Blues' but was also the author of the script of her
only film. Cora Fisher is an even more surprising name.
She and her husband, Lonnie, managed the Moses
Stokes show in which Clarence was working in 1912
when Bessie joined it. If Bessie did mention those two
names she was answering a different question, one

about the gratitude she felt; the techniques and phrasing she used hardly derive from either.

Whether or not Bessie knew how much she learned from her, it is Ma Rainey's throaty shout that can sometimes be mistaken for Bessie. Her singing was in the air as Bessie began; and Bessie always recognized instinctively what she could use. Her own raw talent was greater, however; and she had a stronger need to invent. Bessie was original in the way Armstrong was. She shaped old melodies to the phrases of her own thought. In 'Careless Love', his cornet and her voice respond to one another with joyous virtuosity.

Bessie knew what the world thought was her place, but she did not accept that place. And so we remember her on her own terms.

I ain't' good-lookin' but I'm somebody's angel child.

We accept her as we learn to accept ourselves.

SELECTED BIBLIOGRAPHY

Odum, H. W., and S. B. Johnson, *Negro Workaday Songs*, University of North Carolina Press, 1926.

Handy, W. C., *Father of the Blues*, New York, Macmillan, 1941.

Hodes, Art, article in *Jazz Record*, September 1947.

Van Vechten, Carl, 'Memories of Bessie Smith', *Jazz Record*, September 1947.

Waters, Ethel, and Charles Samuels, *His Eye Is on the Sparrow*, New York, Doubleday, 1950.

Shapiro, Nat, and Nat Hentoff, *Hear Me Talkin' To Ya*, New York, Rinehart, 1955.

Shapiro, Nat, and Nat Hentoff, *The Jazz Makers*, New York, Rinehart, 1957.

Albee, Edward, *The Death of Bessie Smith*, New York, Coward-McCann, 1960.

Bechet, Sidney, *Treat it Gentle*, New York, Hill and Wang, 1960.

Jones, LeRoi, *Blues People*, New York, William Morrow, 1963.

BESSIE SMITH

Bradford, Perry, *Born With the Blues*, New York, Oak Publications, 1965.

Schuller, Gunther, *Early Jazz*, New York, Oxford University Press, 1968.

Oliver, Paul, *The Story of the Blues*, New York, Chilton Book Co., 1969.

Chilton, John, *Who's Who of Jazz*, London, Bloomsbury Book Shop, 1970.

Baxter, Derrick S., *Ma Rainey and the Classic Blues Singers*, New York, Stein and Day, 1970.

Schiffman, Jack, *Uptown – The Story of Harlem's Apollo Theater*, New York, Cowles Book Co., 1971.

Albertson, Chris, *Bessie*, New York, Stein and Day, 1971.

Jones, Hettie, *Big Star Fallin' Mama*, New York, Viking, 1974.

McKee, Margaret, and Fred Chisenhall, *Beale Black and Blue*, Louisiana State University Press, 1981.

SELECTED DISCOGRAPHY

The following long-playing albums relate directly or indirectly to Bessie Smith.

Bessie Smith

THE WORLD'S GREATEST BLUES SINGER (Columbia GP-33): Down Hearted Blues; Gulf Coast Blues; Aggravatin' Papa; Beale Street Mama; Baby Won't You Please Come Home; Oh, Daddy; T'ain't Nobody's Bizness If I Do; Keeps on a-Rainin'; Mama's Got the Blues; Outside of That; Bleeding Hearted Blues; Lady Luck Blues; Yodelling Blues; Midnight Blues; If You Don't, I Know Who Will; Nobody in Town Can Bake a Sweet Jelly Roll like Mine; See If I'll Care; Baby Have Pity on Me; On Revival Day; Moan, You Mourners; Hustlin' Dan; Black Mountain Blues; In the House Blues; Long Old Road; Blue Blues; Shipwreck Blues; Need a Little Sugar in My Bowl; Safety Mama; Do Your Duty; Gimme a Pigfoot; Take Me for a Buggy Ride; Down in the Dumps.

ANY WOMAN'S BLUES (Columbia G 30126): Jail House Blues;

St Louis Gal; Sam Jones Blues; Graveyard Dream Blues; Cemetery Blues; Far Away Blues; I'm Going Back to My Used to Be; Whoa, Tillie, Take Your Time; My Sweetie Went Away; Any Woman's Blues; Chicago Bound Blues; Mistreating Daddy; Frosty Morning Blues; Haunted House Blues; Eavesdropper's Blues; Easy Come, Easy Go Blues; I'm Wild About That Thing; You've Got to Give Me Some; Kitchen Man; I've Got What It Takes; Nobody Knows You When You're Down and Out; Take It Right Back; He's Got Me Goin'; It Makes My Love Come Down; Wasted Life Blues; Dirty No-Gooder's Blues; Blue Spirit Blues; Worn Out Papa Blues; You Don't Understand; Don't Cry Baby; Keep It to Yourself; New Orleans Hop Scop Blues.

EMPTY BED BLUES (Columbia G 30450): Sorrowful Blues; Pinchbacks – Take 'Em Away; Rocking Chair Blues; Ticket Agent, Ease Your Window Down; Boweavil Blues; Hateful Blues; Frankie Blues; Moonshine Blues; Lou'siana Low Down Blues; Mountain Top Blues; Workhorse Blues; House Tent Blues; Salt Water Blues; Rainy Weather Blues; Weeping Willow Blues; The Bye Bye Blues; I Used to Be Your Sweet Mama; I'd Rather Be Dead and Buried in My Grave; Standin' in the Rain Blues; It Won't Be You; Spider Man Blues; Empty Bed Blues (Parts I and II); Put It Right Here; Yes Indeed He Do!; Devil's Gonna Get You; You Ought to Be Ashamed; Washwoman's Blues; Slow and Easy Man; Poor Man's Blues; Please Help Me Get Him off My Mind; Me and My Gin.

THE EMPRESS (Columbia G 30818): Sing Sing Prison Blues; Follow the Deal on Down; Sinful Blues; Woman's Trouble Blues; Love Me Daddy Blues; Dying Gambler's Blues; St Louis Blues; Reckless Blues; Sobbin' Hearted Blues; Cold in Hand Blues; You've Been a Good Ole Wagon; Cake Walking Babies; Yellow

Dog Blues; Soft Pedal Blues; Dixie Flyer Blues; Nashville Woman's Blues; Mean Old Bedbug Blues; A Good Man Is Hard to Find; Homeless Blues; Looking for My Man Blues; Dyin' by the Hour; Foolish Man Blues; Thinking Blues; Pickpocket Blues; Muddy Water; There'll Be a Hot Time in the Old Town Tonight; Trombone Cholly; Send Me to the 'Lectric Chair; Them's Graveyard Words; Hot Springs Blues; Sweet Mistreater; Lock and Key.

NOBODY'S BLUES BUT MINE (Columbia G 31093): Careless Love Blues; J. C. Holmes Blues; I Ain't Goin' to Play Second Fiddle; He's Gone Blues; Nobody's Blues But Mine; I Ain't Got Nobody; My Man Blues; New Gulf Coast Blues; Florida Bound Blues; At the Christmas Ball; I've Been Mistreated and I Don't Like It; Red Mountain Blues; Golden Rule Blues; Lonesome Desert Blues; Them 'Has Been' Blues; Squeeze Me; What's the Matter Now?; I Want Ev'ry Bit of It; Jazzbo Brown from Memphis Town; The Gin House Blues; Money Blues; Baby Doll; Hard Driving Papa; Lost Your Head Blues; Hard Time Blues; Honey Man Blues; One and Two Blues; Young Woman's Blues; Preachin' the Blues; Back Water Blues; After You've Gone; Alexander's Ragtime Band.

Ma Rainey

THE IMMORTAL MA RAINEY (Milestone MLP-2001): Jealous Hearted Blues; Cell Bound Blues; Army Camp Harmony Blues; Explainin' the Blues; Night Time Blues; 'Fore Day Honry Scat; Tough and Tumble Blues; Memphis Bound Blues; Slave to the Blues; Bessemer Bound Blues; Slow Driving Moan; Gone Daddy Blues.

BLAME IT ON THE BLUES (Milestone MLP-2008): Chain Gang Blues; Wringing and Twisting Blues; Dead Drunk Blues; Ma Rainey's Black Bottom; New Boweavil Blues; Moonshine Blues; Deep Moanin' Blues; Daddy, Goodbye Blues; Tough Luck Blues; Blame It on the Blues; Sweet Rough Man; Black Eye Blues.

DOWN IN THE BASEMENT (Milestone MLP-2017): Mountain Jack Blues; Broken Hearted Blues; Down in the Basement; Trust No Man; Morning Hour Blues; Blues, Oh Blues; Oh, Papa Blues; Black Cat Hoot Owl Blues; Hear Me Talkin' To You; Prove It on Me Blues; Victim of the Blues; Sleep Talking Blues; Runaway Blues; Leaving This Morning.

BLUES THE WORLD FORGOT (Biograph BLP-12001): Booze and Blues; Toad Frog Blues; Louisiana Hoo Doo Blues; Stormy Sea Blues; Levee Camp Moan; Titanic Man Blues; Broken Soul Blues; Weeping Woman Blues; Misery Blues; Blues the World Forgot (Parts I and II); Travelling Blues.

OH, MY BABE BLUES (Biograph BLP-12011): Jealousy Blues; Shave 'Em Dry; Farewell Daddy Blues; Oh, My Babe Blues; Soon This Morning; Don't Fish in My Sea; Countin' the Blues; Sissy Blues; Log Camp Blues; Hustlin' Blues; Ma and Pa Poorhouse Blues; Big Feeling Blues.

QUEEN OF THE BLUES (Biograph BLP-12032): Sad Lick Blues; Boweavil Blues; Barrel House Blues; Those All Night Long Blues; Moonshine Blues; Last Minute Blues; Southern Blues; Wailing Blues; Lost Wandering Blues; Dream Blues; Honey, Where You Been So Long; Ya Da Do; Those Dogs of Mine; Lucky Rock Blues; South Bound Blues; Lawd, Send Me a Man Blues.

Ethel Waters

OH, DADDY! (Biograph BLP-12022): Oh, Daddy!; Down Home Blues; One-Man Nan; There'll Be Some Changes Made; At the New Jump Steady Ball; Oh, Joe, Play That Trombone; Memphis Man; Midnight Blues; That Da Da Strain; Georgia Blues; You Can't Do What My Last Man Did; Ethel Sing 'Em; Sweet Man; Craving Blues.

JAZZIN' BABIES' BLUES (Biograph BLP-12026): The New York Glide; At the New Jump Steady Ball; Dying with the Blues; Kiss Your Pretty Baby Nice; Jazzin' Babies' Blues; King Lovin' Blues; Broken Baby; Ain't Goin' to Marry; You'll Need Me When I'm Long Gone; I Want Somebody All My Own; Black Spatch Blues; One Sweet Letter from You.

ON STAGE AND SCREEN 1925–1940 (Columbia CL-2792): Dinah; I'm Coming, Virginia; Am I Blue?; Birmingham Bertha; You're Lucky to Me; Memories of You; You Can't Stop Me from Loving You; Stormy Weather; Heatwave; Harlem on My Mind; Hottentot Potentate; Thief in the Night; Taking a Chance on Love; Honey in the Honeycomb; Cabin in the Sky; Love Turned the Light Out.

ACKNOWLEDGEMENTS

Grateful acknowledgement is made for permission to reprint excerpts from the following lyrics:

'Dirty No-Gooder's Blues' by Bessie Smith, © 1929, 1974 Frank Music Corp.; © Renewed 1957 Frank Music Corp. International copyright secured. All rights reserved. Used by permission.

'Down in the Dumps' by Wesley Wilson & Leola P. Wilson, © 1958, 1974 Frank Music Corp. International copyright secured. All rights reserved. Used by permission.

'Please Help Me Get Him Off My Mind' by Bessie Smith, © 1928, 1974 Frank Music Corp.; © Renewed 1956 Frank Music Corp. International copyright secured. All rights reserved. Used by permission.

'Reckless Blues' by Bessie Smith, © 1925, 1974 Frank Music Corp.; © Renewed 1953 Frank Music Corp. International copyright secured. All rights reserved. Used by permission.

'Sorrowful Blues' by Bessie Smith, © 1924 Frank Music Corp.; © Renewed 1952 Frank Music Corp. International copyright secured. All rights reserved. Used by permission.

'Young Woman's Blues' by Bessie Smith, © 1927, 1974

ACKNOWLEDGEMENTS

Frank Music Corp.; © Renewed 1955 Frank Music Corp. International copyright secured. All rights reserved. Used by permission.

'Nobody Knows You When You're Down and Out', words and music by Jimmy Cox, © 1923, 1929 by MCA Music, a division of MCA Inc., New York, N.Y. Copyright renewed. All rights reserved. Used by permission. Reproduced courtesy of EMI Music Ltd., London WC2H 0LD, for the British Commonwealth, excluding Canada and Australasia.

'Tain't Nobody's Biz-ness If I Do', words and music by Porter Grainger and Everett Robbins, © 1922 by MCA Music, a division of MCA Inc., New York, N.Y. Copyright renewed. All rights reserved. Used by permission. © Lawrence Wright Music Company Limited for the World, excluding USA, Canada and Australasia.

A CHOICE OF PENGUINS

☐ **The Complete Penguin Stereo Record and Cassette Guide**
Greenfield, Layton and March   £7.95

A new edition, now including information on compact discs. 'One of the few indispensables on the record collector's bookshelf' – *Gramophone*

☐ **Selected Letters of Malcolm Lowry**
Edited by Harvey Breit and Margerie Bonner Lowry £5.95

'Lowry emerges from these letters not only as an extremely interesting man, but also a lovable one' – Philip Toynbee

☐ **The First Day on the Somme**
Martin Middlebrook   £3.95

1 July 1916 was the blackest day of slaughter in the history of the British Army. 'The soldiers receive the best service a historian can provide: their story told in their own words' – *Guardian*

☐ **A Better Class of Person** **John Osborne**   £1.95

The playwright's autobiography, 1929–56. 'Splendidly enjoyable' – John Mortimer. 'One of the best, richest and most bitterly truthful autobiographies that I have ever read' – Melvyn Bragg

☐ **The Winning Streak** **Goldsmith and Clutterbuck**   £2.95

Marks & Spencer, Saatchi & Saatchi, United Biscuits, GEC . . . The UK's top companies reveal their formulas for success, in an important and stimulating book that no British manager can afford to ignore.

☐ **The First World War** **A. J. P. Taylor**   £3.95

'He manages in some 200 illustrated pages to say almost everything that is important . . . A special text . . . a remarkable collection of photographs' – *Observer*

A CHOICE OF PENGUINS

☐ **Man and the Natural World** **Keith Thomas** £4.95

Changing attitudes in England, 1500–1800. 'An encyclopedic study of man's relationship to animals and plants . . . a book to read again and again' – Paul Theroux, *Sunday Times* Books of the Year

☐ **Jean Rhys: Letters 1931–66**
Edited by Francis Wyndham and Diana Melly £3.95

'Eloquent and invaluable . . . her life emerges, and with it a portrait of an unexpectedly indomitable figure' – Marina Warner in the *Sunday Times*

☐ **The French Revolution** **Christopher Hibbert** £4.50

'One of the best accounts of the Revolution that I know . . . Mr Hibbert is outstanding' – J. H. Plumb in the *Sunday Telegraph*

☐ **Isak Dinesen** **Judith Thurman** £4.95

The acclaimed life of Karen Blixen, 'beautiful bride, disappointed wife, radiant lover, bereft and widowed woman, writer, sibyl, Scheherazade, child of Lucifer, Baroness; always a unique human being . . . an assiduously researched and finely narrated biography' – *Books & Bookmen*

☐ **The Amateur Naturalist**
Gerald Durrell with Lee Durrell £4.95

'Delight . . . on every page . . . packed with authoritative writing, learning without pomposity . . . it represents a real bargain' – *The Times Educational Supplement*. 'What treats are in store for the average British household' – *Daily Express*

☐ **When the Wind Blows** **Raymond Briggs** £2.95

'A visual parable against nuclear war: all the more chilling for being in the form of a strip cartoon' – *Sunday Times*. 'The most eloquent anti-Bomb statement you are likely to read' – *Daily Mail*

A CHOICE OF PENGUINS

☐ **_The Diary of Virginia Woolf_**
Edited by Quentin Bell and Anne Olivier Bell

'As an account of the intellectual and cultural life of our century, Virginia Woolf's diaries are invaluable; as the record of one bruised and unquiet mind, they are unique' – Peter Ackroyd in the _Sunday Times_

☐ Volume One	£4.50
☐ Volume Two	£4.50
☐ Volume Three	£4.95
☐ Volume Four	£5.50
☐ Volume Five	£5.95

These books should be available at all good bookshops or news-agents, but if you live in the UK or the Republic of Ireland and have difficulty in getting to a bookshop, they can be ordered by post. Please indicate the titles required and fill in the form below.

NAME _____ BLOCK CAPITALS

ADDRESS _____

_____

_____

Enclose a cheque or postal order payable to The Penguin Bookshop to cover the total price of books ordered, plus 50p for postage. Readers in the Republic of Ireland should send £1R equivalent to the sterling prices, plus 67p for postage. Send to: The Penguin Bookshop, 54/56 Bridlesmith Gate, Nottingham, NG1 2GP.

You can also order by phoning (0602) 599295, and quoting your Barclaycard or Access number.

Every effort is made to ensure the accuracy of the price and availability of books at the time of going to press, but it is sometimes necessary to increase prices and in these circumstances retail prices may be shown on the covers of books which may differ from the prices shown in this list or elsewhere. This list is not an offer to supply any book.

This order service is only available to residents in the UK and the Republic of Ireland.